DB CARGO LOCOMOTIVES AND STOCK IN THE UK

John Jackson

AMBERLEY

First published 2018

Amberley Publishing
The Hill, Stroud
Gloucestershire, GL5 4EP

www.amberley-books.com

Copyright © John Jackson, 2018

The right of John Jackson to be identified as
the Author of this work has been asserted in
accordance with the Copyrights, Designs and
Patents Act 1988.

ISBN 978 1 4456 8296 9 (print)
ISBN 978 1 4456 8297 6 (ebook)

British Library Cataloguing in Publication Data.
A catalogue record for this book is available from
the British Library.

Origination by Amberley Publishing.
Printed in the UK.

Introduction

As the title suggests, this book takes a look at the position DB Cargo holds within today's railway. In common with many other rail operating companies, much has happened in its brief history. That history spans two decades, which commenced with its formation from out of the ashes of what was then British Rail. Since then, the company has undergone several re-brandings and name changes. To an enthusiast looking on, it also appears to have undergone several changes of direction.

Before we take a brief look at what happened to this company in those intervening years, let me take you back to one particular moment that will count among the most important, not only when writing the history of DB Cargo, but of our railways generally as they moved into the twenty-first century.

The date was 29 August 1998. The place was Toton Depot, on the borders of Nottinghamshire and Derbyshire. The occasion was my first glimpse of a Class 66 – or a 'Shed' to many – as I saw GM-built and newly delivered No. 66001. The locomotive was on display there together with two more examples, Nos 66003 and 66004. Even more exciting was the pledge that a total of 250 locos were on order. That figure rises to 280 if the additional, smaller order for thirty Class 67s is included in the calculation.

I genuinely believed we were about to witness a new dawn in the history of our railways, and conveyance of rail-borne freight in particular. Now, as I write this some twenty years after that moment, I feel that the jury is still out as to what, if anything, this company has achieved.

But more of that later. Let's take a look at how DB Cargo got to where it is today. As I said, its roots were in the selling off process of the nationalised rail freight business as the government of the day sought to place our railways in private hands.

In 1995, a company called North & South Railways was involved in the bidding process for a number of former British Rail businesses offered for sale. Rail Express Systems was successfully acquired at the end of that year. This was the sector responsible primarily for rail-based postal traffic, together with the operation of the Royal Train. The deal brought with it around 150 locos and just short of 700 postal vans.

The following year, several further rail freight companies were acquired, with Loadhaul, Mainline Freight and TransRail Freight joining their stable. That deal brought with it considerable assets: almost 1,000 locos and approaching 20,000 wagons.

These individual companies, or 'brands', were retained for a while, but by 1996 the English, Welsh & Scottish Railway name and EWS branding were unveiled. Within a few months the staff and other assets had been absorbed into the new, enlarged company. This company was a consortium led by the US-based Wisconsin Central Transportation Corporation (WCTC).

The government's disposal of the remaining sector, Railfreight Distribution (RfD), was more problematic. Since the days of the Beeching Report in the 1960s, it was inevitable that the focus for rail movement of freight would be via full trainloads for one customer and not individual wagonloads for one or more businesses. In the run up to privatisation, Railfeight Distribution's portfolio included the Speedlink brand, together with a variety of other traffic as diverse as MoD, automotive, china clay and timber, to name just a few. Speedlink's problem in a nutshell was that it bore fixed costs but variable revenue, with these trains all too often conveying too small a level of traffic to break even.

During the mid-1990s, this sector was also responsible for Freightliner and Channel Tunnel movements, including the recently procured fleet of thirty Class 92 locomotives. In 1995, Freightliner assets were transferred into a new company, Freightliner Ltd, which shortly afterwards became the Freightliner Group.

Meanwhile, towards the end of 1996, EWS was named as the successful bidder for the loss-making RfD. This loss-making business was eventually sold to EWS the following year with the new company receiving various grants and subsidies. It also meant defeat for the government's attempt to create a rail freight marketplace where open competition between private enterprises could thrive. At the time of this sale, EWS's share of the total rail freight business was estimated to be between 80 and 90 per cent.

In the following year, this new business boasted a total of 1,200 locos, the 20,000 wagons referred to above and a total workforce of around 7,000. Steps to reduce the latter were inevitable and volunteers for redundancy were sought.

Turning to the loco and wagon assets, the company considered that the majority of the locos it had inherited from British Rail were either life expired or too expensive to maintain. Many were simply empty shells – or 'Christmas Trees' as they were known in the industry – hence the order for Class 66 and 67 locos referred to above. Once delivery was completed, these locos would replace the majority of the inherited classes of locomotives. Some of these were to see transfer abroad, while others remain side-lined here in the UK to this day. A similar picture was to emerge in respect of the wagon fleet.

In 1998, EWS took over the rail division of National Power, including six Class 59 locos and yet more wagons. In 2001, WCTC's share in EWS was acquired by Canadian National and then came the news in 2003 that the Royal Mail was to switch almost its entire postal operation to road transport.

A couple of years later, Euro Cargo Rail, a recently formed French subsidiary of EWS, received a total of sixty Class 66s from the UK-based fleet of 250. Some of these locos have occasionally returned to the UK for attention at DB Cargo's Toton Depot.

In 2007, Deutsche Bahn agreed to purchase the EWS business. Initially, the company branding remained unchanged, but in 2009 EWS was renamed DB Schenker Rail UK.

In another move, similar to the French loco transfers above, a batch of fifteen Class 66s was transferred to DB Schenker Polska in 2011. Since then, however, none of these locos has returned to the UK. The combined French and Polish transfers reduced the original UK fleet of 250 Class 66s by roughly a third.

To bring this brief history up to date, in March 2016 the company was renamed DB Cargo UK. The familiar 'large numbered' maroon and gold-liveried EWS locomotives have given way to DB red as more locomotives pass through the paintshops. As an aside, my wife, on seeing her first Shed in that familiar maroon colour scheme and gold and large lettering, christened the company 'Elegant with Style'!

Later, in 2016, the company highlighted the obvious downturn in the movement of coal and, to a lesser extent, steel by rail in the UK. DB Cargo cited the early closure of coal-fired power stations as a key factor. Indeed, it is suggested that all movement of coal to power stations will have ceased by the mid-2020s. The word redundancies was again mentioned in its press release.

If I was to listen to the 'experts' to be found at the end of station platforms, you would think that this company has no future. But – and it is an important but – I have tried to confine what is written here to known facts and not speculation.

Those fires were fuelled again during 2017. First, the railway press confirmed that Wabtec had acquired a total of twenty Class 60s from DB Cargo. Most of these locos have languished for many years in the railway graveyard that is Toton Yard. Only time will tell as to what their future holds. But the sale of a further ten Class 66 locos did definitely go ahead, with their acquisition by GBRf taking place at the end of the year.

Perhaps more importantly than individual locos and their futures, DB Cargo seems to be losing more traffic to its competitors than it is gaining from them, but maybe this is just my perception.

And so, that brings us to this present-day look at the company's locos and rolling stock. Inevitably, the 'core' fleet of Class 66s features prominently on the pages that follow, but we also take a look at their other diesel locos, particularly Class 60 and 67s. In addition, the company still retains a dwindling fleet of electric locos on its books. Examples of Class 90 and 92 are also featured here.

We also take a look at some of the various types of wagons in use for DB Cargo and its customers today. Many hundreds of wagons have been adapted to meet today's requirements; many more have faced the cutters' equipment, and continue to do so, particularly in the former freight strongholds of North East England and South Wales. For example, purpose-built biomass wagons have replaced their fleet of coal hoppers (HTAs), while many of the latter now find use on stone and aggregate traffic.

At the end of 2017, DB Cargo announced a substantial investment in trialling a new wagon, designated as HRA, for this traffic. In an attempt to make best use of its redundant HTA coal hoppers, a shorter length prototype was developed in collaboration with W. H. Davis of Shirebrook. DB Cargo revealed plans to reduce the length of some 110 of these coal hoppers by approximately 20 per cent without impacting on the gross weight carried by each wagon, and this should see more individual wagons within each trainload. Figures of twenty-seven HRAs being equivalent to twenty-two HTAs per train have been mentioned.

As is evidenced towards the end of this book, DB Cargo's operating licence is also called upon in running charter services using steam power. The company is one of the few that offer this main line running, albeit only using steam locos fitted with air brakes.

So, as I complete this introduction, it continues to be a case of 'good news, bad news' for this company's future. On the one hand, they have recently signed a contract extension to handle Malcolm Logistics' Anglo-Scottish traffic until 2020. Their own website proudly claims that this rail flow saves an estimated 13 million road miles per year. Yet, at the same time, the flow that I have watched, almost since childhood, running between Peak Forest and Bletchley is now in competitors' hands. Freightliner recently took over this operation, bringing a green Class 66/6 to the Marston Vale line in place of the red 66 and, before that, an EWS Class 60. We live in changing times.

As always, I hope you enjoy your journey browsing through these pages as much as I have enjoyed compiling them!

John Jackson

These two photographs capture one of the most important milestones in the history of our privatised railway. The weekend of 29 and 30 August 1998 was, for many enthusiasts, the first chance to see several examples of the first newly delivered Class 66s, including No. 66001 shown here. This was one of the highlights on display at the last public open day to be held at Toton Depot.

While pioneer No. 66001 had arrived at Immingham Docks some four months earlier, at the Toton open day it was joined by No. 66003 (seen here), No. 66004 and No. 66005. These brand-new locos had been delivered via Newport Docks just a day or two earlier. Sister loco No. 66002 was absent as it was undergoing trials at Pueblo, USA, prior to rolling out the proposed fleet of 250 locos.

These trials with No. 66002 were successful and the go ahead was given for the full production run. Impressively, the last loco of the production batch of 250 locos, namely No. 66250, was delivered to the UK just over two years later. It is seen here, around fifteen years later, approaching Long Buckby on 15 January 2015. It had only just left Daventry International Rail Freight Terminal on a southbound van working to Dollands Moor for onward movement via the Channel Tunnel.

In recent years, the EWS maroon and gold livery has given way to DB Cargo's new image. The red colour scheme continues to be applied to an increasing number of locos, including No. 66085, seen here. The loco is heading east through Manea on 12 December 2017, working an intermodal from Wakefield Euro Terminal to Felixstowe.

In sharp contrast, this scene shows DB Cargo's loco maintenance hub at Toton. It was taken on a snowy day, 18 March 2018, and shows the row of stored Class 60 locomotives. The weather changes, the seasons come and go, but this timeless view of unwanted locomotives, less than thirty years old, hasn't changed for many years.

The Training Compound at Toton has been home to a number of classes deemed obsolete by their owners. Several examples are shown in this photograph taken on 12 January 2014. Mainline-liveried No. 58023 is seen sandwiched between several examples of the company's Class 08 diesel shunters.

Crewe Electric Depot is also something of a graveyard, particularly for the company's electric locomotives. Contrasting liveries are on display in this shot taken on 1 October 2017. Nearest the camera is No. 90033 in Railfreight Distribution colours (a legacy of its British Rail days), with No. 90023 behind in faded maroon and gold.

Examples of DB Cargo's fleet of Class 67s are also having their maroon and gold liveries replaced. On 22 February 2017, EWS-liveried No. 67008 stands at Doncaster.

On 29 June 2017, No. 67028 stands in almost the same location. By then this locomotive had been outshopped in DB Cargo red livery.

The new company colours are also being applied to Class 90 electric locos. On 19 June 2017, one of those not yet repainted, No. 90037 *Spirit of Dagenham*, is seen in its EWS livery as it heads south through Nuneaton on a Crewe to Wembley light engine move.

In contrast, on 18 December 2017, new-liveried No. 90018 leads No. 90028 through Nuneaton on a Mossend to Daventry intermodal. In December 2015, loco No. 90018 had been named *The Pride of Bellshill*.

At the end of 2017, DB Cargo sold ten of its Class 66 locomotives to GBRf. Included in that sale was No. 66238. It is seen here in its DB Cargo days, on 27 May 2016, heading south through Loughborough on a steel working from Margam (South Wales) to Corby in Northamptonshire.

Serious loco accidents among the Class 66 fleet have, thankfully, been few and far between. However, No. 66048, and its Inverness to Mossend intermodal, became derailed at Carrbridge, in the Scottish Highlands, during an extremely cold winter's day in January 2010. It was eventually withdrawn and its final resting place was to be Electromotive's depot at Longport, near Stoke-on-Trent. Prior to removal, it is seen here 'incognito' at Toton on 23 January 2016.

This busy scene at Peak Forest in Derbyshire shows DB Cargo at its best. Old and new liveries are in evidence on 21 March 2018 as No. 66171 passes two sister locos, which are both employed in loading their rakes at Dove Holes Quarry.

Following the sale of ten locos to Colas, DB Cargo retains ninety Class 60 locos on its books, although the majority are out of use at Toton. Around fifteen locos could be regarded as active on a daily basis. One of these, No. 60066, has been repainted in a unique livery: 'Drax – powering tomorrow'. It is seen here at Oakley, north of Bedford, having assisted No. 66135 on a Bletchley to Toton working on 30 September 2017.

The remainder of the regular active fleet of Class 60s has been outshopped in DB Cargo red livery. On 16 April 2018, No. 60020 *The Willows* awaits its next duty, having spent the weekend stabled in Tees Yard, near Middlesbrough.

As already mentioned, Toton is the nerve centre for DB Cargo's locomotive servicing and stabling. On 19 April 2017, four examples of the class are grouped outside the north end of the depot itself. From left to right these are Nos 66144, 66160, 66174 and 66022. The latter is a French example of the class, temporarily back at the depot for attention. It returned to France via the Channel Tunnel the following month.

DB Cargo no longer uses its ageing fleet of Class 08 diesel shunters; instead, it now opts to perform any yard shunting required at Toton (and elsewhere) using either a Class 60 or Class 66 locomotive. On 19 April 2017, it was the turn of No. 60017 to perform these duties.

On several occasions DB Cargo has opted to brand its locos in the house colours of its customers. One Class 90 has been branded twice in the space of two years. No. 90024 is seen stabled on an additional Christmas post working at Carlisle on 17 December 2015. At the time it was sporting the colours of First ScotRail, reflecting a time when the company was contracted to haul Anglo-Scottish sleeper services.

Two years later, on 3 October 2017, No. 90024 is again seen at Carlisle. On this occasion, it is working alongside sister loco No. 90019 on a Coatbridge to Daventry intermodal. By that date, it had received Malcolm Logistics branding.

The dramatic downturn in coal traffic has hit the rail freight operators hard, and this particular working through the Midlands is therefore something of a rarity. It is a DB Cargo working between Margam and Scunthorpe destined for the steel works there. Here, the empties are seen returning south through Sileby on 12 April 2018 behind No. 66138.

Biomass has replaced coal as the fuel source at Drax Power Station with trains delivering around 20,000 tons of wood pellets each day. DB Cargo operates services from the ports of Hull and Immingham into the power station. On 19 April 2018, No. 66172 *Paul Melleney* approaches Sudforth Lane crossing (at Beal in North Yorkshire) with a return rake of empties for Immingham.

DB Cargo has also seen a downturn in the amount of steel traffic that it handles. One surviving service links Tata's steel terminal at Round Oak, Brierley Hill (in the West Midlands), with its plants in South Wales. On 21 February 2018, No. 66011 hauls a mixed rake of wagons through Severn Tunnel Junction on its return to Margam.

The movement of aggregates for the construction industry is another important source of revenue for DB Cargo, and none more so than from the Tarmac-owned quarry at Mountsorrel in Leicestershire. On 15 February 2018, No. 66015 works a rake of empties through Leicester on the return leg from Elstow (south of Bedford) to Mountsorrel.

Between 2001 and 2002, 1,162 coal hoppers, classified as HTAs, were built for DB Cargo at Thrall's York Works. On 25 September 2012, loaded HTA wagon No. 310371 is seen passing through Barnetby.

DB Cargo's displaced HTAs, redundant after the downturn in coal traffic, have seen alternative use on the company's stone traffic, notably out of Peak Forest in Derbyshire. In this view, wagon No. 311077 waits in the yard at Peak Forest on 31 October 2015.

In 2013, W. H. Davis at Shirebrook commenced building new hoppers for Drax Power Station's biomass traffic. These wagons, designated IIAs, are covered to prevent the compressed wood pellets getting wet and becoming unusable. These newly delivered wagons were numbered in the RIV series and here wagon No. 7006980473 passes through Scunthorpe in a DB Cargo-hauled rake bound for Drax.

The HTAs, in part, were replacements for the Merry-Go-Round (MGR) coal hoppers built half a century before. Over 11,000 hoppers were built from the mid-1960s. The majority of these wagons were designated HAAs, and they were mostly built at Shildon Works. Wagon No. 350002, pictured here, was the first of the production run; it is preserved and sits proudly on a plinth at the entrance to DB Cargo's Knottingley Depot.

Class 60s continue to find regular employment on the tank traffic between South Humberside and Kingsbury (near Tamworth). On 3 May 2017, No. 60054 works a rake of returning empties through Barnetby heading to Humber Oil Refinery.

On 28 March 2018, No. 60017 is seen on the same working. This time the empties are heading east through Lincoln station.

DB Cargo handles infrastructure work for a variety of projects on behalf of Network Rail. On 9 March 2018, No. 66116 is seen heading through Leicester on a Sharnbrook Junction to Toton working. The train had run in connection with track improvement and re-instatement work further south on the Midland Main Line.

On 29 April 2017, No. 66114 is seen leaving Eastleigh Yard with a rake of loaded ballast wagons. The trainload of fresh ballast is heading for an engineering project in the Horsham area.

Major improvement work is taking place at Derby station through 2018, including additional platform building and track realignment. Ahead of this building work No. 66170 is seen in the station area on 10 January 2018. It is at the head of a spoil removal train.

For many years, DB Cargo has operated regular infrastructure trains between the yards at Toton and Bescot (West Midlands). These workings are often also used to incorporate loco moves between these two locations. On 14 July 2017, No. 66116 is seen hauling the Toton-bound working through Burton-on-Trent. On this occasion, the opportunity has been taken to move Greater Anglia electric loco No. 90001 to Toton for repaint work.

The majority of MGR coal hoppers belonging to DB Cargo were deemed life expired and sold for scrap. Around 1,000 underframes were, however, used as donors for the fleet of 'coalfish' engineering wagons, designated MHAs. Wagon No. 394527 stands in Derby loaded with spoil for removal from the work site.

A similar project saw over 200 further wagons converted from redundant Shell oil tank wagons. These were primarily for engineers' traffic and were designated MTAs. One such example, No. 395220, is seen at Toton Yard in the consist of a loaded rake.

Another MHA wagon, No. 394321, is seen through Bedford in the consist of a rake of loaded ballast wagons, ahead of its load being dropped on the Marston Vale branch between there and Bletchley.

The sole long-term resident of Worcester Yard is MHA No. 394247. It has languished here since at least May 2012 (my first recorded sighting of it here) as if staking a company claim to its environs. This photograph was taken on 7 November 2017.

The six Class 59/2 locos, built in the mid-1990s, have been on DB Cargo's books since 1998. On 11 May 2017, No. 59203 arrives at Acton Yard with a rake of empties returning from Chelmsford.

Sister loco No. 59202 *Alan Meddows Taylor MD Mendip Rail Limited* was seen on railtour duties a few days later, working the return leg of 'The Cornishman' from Penzance to Paddington. On 29 May 2017, it is seen arriving at Par station in Cornwall. Earlier the westbound working had been in the hands of steam loco No. 60163, *Tornado*.

On 22 September 2015, No. 59202 is on more familiar duties as it heads through Upper Holloway on the North London Line. This time its rake of empties is on a Dagenham to Acton working.

These 59/2 locos can mainly be seen on workings to and from the quarries in the South West. On 13 July 2016, No. 59201 is seen heading west through Reading station, returning a long rake of empties to the quarry at Merehead in Somerset.

For many years DB Cargo has provided Class 67 locos at several strategic locations on the East Coast Main Line (ECML) for use in emergency rescues, mainly for other operators. These 'Thunderbird' locations include King's Cross station, where No. 67030 is seen on 3 April 2017.

These locos are also usually found stabled at the northern extreme of the electrified stretch of the ECML, namely Edinburgh Waverley. On 8 April 2015, No. 67021 is found performing this duty.

Further south, on 13 June 2013, it's the turn of No. 67016 to be stabled at Newcastle's Central station.

On 5 January 2018, No. 67010 has just arrived at Doncaster's West Yard, complete with a rake of Virgin Trains East Coast stock and loco, which it has dragged from the north. Electric loco No. 91102 is out of view on the rear and Driving Vehicle Trailer (DVT) No. 82200 is attached to the Class 67.

With fierce competition among the various rail freight companies, inevitably there are geographical pockets of the country where DB Cargo fairs best. At the time of writing, South Wales remains a stronghold, particularly within the steel sector. In a typical scene on 22 February 2018, No. 66092 passes west through Cardiff station with a mixed rake of steel wagons from Newport Docks to Margam Yard.

On the previous day, No. 66182 heads through Cardiff in the opposite direction with a rake of steel coils being tripped from Margam to Llanwern.

On 12 November 2017, Nos 66006 and 66025 are both at work at the western end of Margam Knuckle Yard. This location is close to the giant steel complex at Port Talbot in South Wales.

On 8 November 2017, No. 66031 waits alongside Severn Tunnel Junction station while working another mixed rake of steel wagons from Round Oak to Margam.

DB Cargo inherited a wide range of steel wagons on railway privatisation. This loaded steel coil carrier, designated BLA and numbered No. 910263, is seen being moved from Port Talbot Steelworks to Margam Knuckle Yard. These steel wagons date from the 1970s and 1980s.

Fairing less well is this steel wagon, designated code BDA and numbered No. 950471, which has just been unloaded at Wolverhampton Steel Terminal and clearly shows evidence of use over almost half a century.

As with the coal sector, DB Cargo has seen a downturn in rail-carried steel. Inevitably, former steel wagons have been adapted for alternative use. One project saw over 200 former steel wagons converted from 2015 onwards. They became bogie box wagons and were re-designated MXAs. The pool included No. 950805, seen here in Doncaster Decoy Yard. The DB red livery quickly earned them the nickname 'lobsters'.

Another prototype conversion from a former steel wagon is No. 910164, designated MVA. This ballast open wagon is currently being trialled. It is seen here in a consist at Acton Yard.

DB Cargo currently provides Class 90 electric locos to cover for non-availability within Virgin Trains East Coast's own fleet of Class 91 electrics. On 31 October 2017, No. 90019 *Multimodal* arrives at Peterborough while working a service from King's Cross to Newark Northgate.

These locos are usually found leading at the 'country end' when leaving King's Cross with a DVT at the 'London' end. This means they are propelling when working south, as seen here on 2 April 2018, as No. 90029 passes through Hitchin heading for London King's Cross.

On 18 February 2018, No. 90039, another example still in former maroon and gold livery, is seen passing Tempsford crossing, near Sandy.

This more unusual working for Virgin Trains East Coast occurred on 13 February 2018. DB Cargo loco No. 90034, on hire, was called upon to move two Class 91 locos, Nos 91105 and 91120, from Bounds Green depot in North London to Doncaster. It is seen here shortly after arrival in the latter's West Yard.

There is no doubt that DB Cargo's competitors move the majority of railborne containers within the UK. DB Cargo does, however, operate a number of intermodal services between ports and inland terminals. One such example is the traffic between the Euro Terminal near Wakefield and the port of Felixstowe. On 8 September 2017, No. 66063 heads through the village of Elmswell with a working heading for the Suffolk port.

DB Cargo also handles services to and from the port of Southampton. On 9 May 2017, No. 66030 is seen passing through Leamington Spa with a working from Trafford Park in Manchester to the South Coast port.

On 23 February 2018, No. 66094 is seen passing Hinksey Yard, near Oxford, with a northbound working from Southampton. This time the destination is the inland terminal at Birch Coppice near Tamworth.

The inland terminal at Trafford Park also sees services operating to and from London Gateway. On 28 June 2017, No. 66160 is seen London-bound as it heads through Stafford.

For a number of years DB Cargo has provided Class 67 locos to sister company Arriva Trains Wales. Indeed, three examples bear the familiar turquoise colour scheme of this operator. The Class 67s are used on workings that link Holyhead with Manchester and Cardiff using a short set of coaches and a DVT. On 26 October 2015, No. 67001 is seen at Manchester Piccadilly.

On 14 July 2015, No. 67002 has just brought the empty coaching stock from Cardiff Canton. It stands at Cardiff Central waiting to form the early evening service to Holyhead.

On 22 February 2018, it's the turn of No. 67020 to work the morning arrival from Holyhead. The train is seen arriving at Cardiff Central around 10.00 with the DVT leading and the loco providing the power, propelling at the rear.

Meanwhile, on 13 February 2018, Arriva-liveried No. 67003 is nowhere near Arriva Trains Wales territory. It is awaiting other duties as the 'Thunderbird' on the East Coast Main Line at Doncaster's West Yard.

Despite competition from Freightliner in particular, DB Cargo still handles a number of freight diagrams to, from and around Teesside. On 18 April 2018, No. 66106 waits to leave the steel complex at Lackenby with a lengthy rake comprising the return working to Scunthorpe.

On the same day, No. 66144 is seen heading towards Grangetown, Teesside, with a return working of just four steel wagons from Skinningrove to Tees Yard.

The previous day finds No. 66142 returning to Teesside, working from Knowsley to Wilton. It is passing Shipton, just north of York. This flow is a long-term contract moving residual waste from Merseyside to the energy-from-waste facility at Middlesbrough.

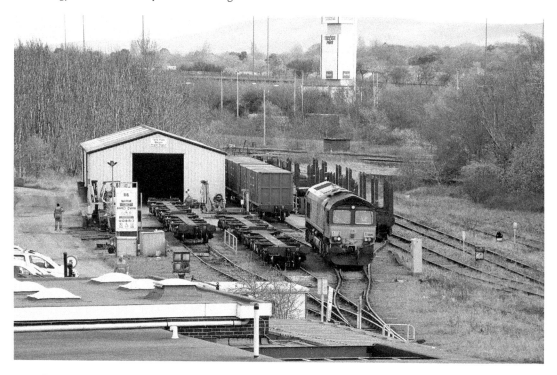

On 18 April 2018, No. 66182 is seen shunting wagons at the wagon repair depot in Tees Yard. Its duties on that day involved moving a couple of wagons dedicated to the above waste flow.

Sometimes things don't go according to plan. DB Cargo regularly delivers the fuel tanks from Lindsey Oil Terminal on Humberside to the depot at Neville Hill in Leeds. It is one of only a handful of freight trains that pass through Leeds station each week. On 11 April 2018, No. 60059 *Swinden Dalesman* approaches the station with its load of four tanks. So far so good…

…. Unfortunately, for reasons unknown, the train came to a stand, blocking the busy (First TransPennine) Platform 15.

Some two hours later assistance came in the form of rescue loco No. 66174, which arrived light engine from the Knottingley area.

The duo eventually cleared Platform 15 around 135 minutes later, completing the short journey to the depot east of Leeds.

As already mentioned, dedicated (Class 08/09) diesel shunters are no longer in use with DB Cargo. Several yards use Class 66 locos for this purpose. One example is at Bescot Yard (in the West Midlands). On 17 May 2017, No. 66075 is performing these duties when photographed adjacent to Bescot Stadium station.

On 8 March 2018, another Class 66 on shunting duties was found in Doncaster's Decoy Yard. The loco in question was No. 66170.

Further south, the Kent yard at Hoo Junction is a hub for engineering traffic, requiring wagon shunting into appropriate rakes, etc. Power for these duties was provided in the form of No. 66230 on 14 December 2017.

Hinksey Yard, near Oxford, is another base for a Class 66 shunter. On 1 May 2017, No. 66024 is stabled here, alongside several Colas Class 70s.

Several rail companies operate services in and out of the important Leicestershire quarry at Mountsorrel. DB Cargo operates to a number of different destinations as well as outstabling Class 66s in the small 'shed' here. On 4 July 2016, No. 66019 is seen in the yard.

On 2 November 2017, No. 66011 is seen heading for Mountsorrel. It is passing Harrowden Junction, north of Wellingborough, on a return empty working from Luton.

On 12 December 2017, No. 66092 is seen heading away from Mountsorrel on a longer distance working. It is heading a rake of loaded wagons as it crosses East Anglia to Trowse, near Norwich. The location is Three Horseshoes level crossing, near Turves in Cambridgeshire.

On 11 February 2017, No. 66119 is also heading to Mountsorrel. It is seen hauling its rake of empties north through Bedford on its return from Radlett, Hertfordshire.

DB Cargo Class 67s also find use on a variety of charter trains. On 21 September 2017, No. 67030 heads through Chesterfield on a charter from King's Cross destined for Barrow Hill and the relaunch following the lottery-funded work on its listed roundhouse.

Later in the day, the return working is seen passing through Nottingham station, with No. 67013 now leading.

Less than three weeks later, No. 67013 has found its way north of the border. On 9 October 2017, it had just brought the Inverness portion of the Highland Sleeper service in to Inverness station. The loco had worked these coaches from Edinburgh Waverley, where this portion had been split from those serving Aberdeen and Fort William.

DB Cargo no longer handles the Fort William and Aberdeen portions of this service. On 6 April 2015, No. 67004, complete with Caledonian Sleeper livery, is seen standing at Fort William before working the southbound service as far as Edinburgh.

With only around fifteen DB Cargo Class 60s in use on any given day, South Wales is usually the base for one or two of them. On 21 February 2018, No. 60054 passes through Cardiff Central on a local steel working from Llanwern to Margam.

The following day, the same loco was diagrammed to work the loaded tanks from Robeston to Westerleigh. This is a diagram that is almost guaranteed to produce a Class 60 at its head. Once again, No. 60054 is seen approaching Cardiff.

On 10 November 2017, No. 60040 *The Territorial Army Centenary* was to be found in Margam Knuckle Yard. It was awaiting transfer to Toton, and hadn't moved for several days.

On 13 November 2017, No. 60007 *The Spirit of Tom Kendell* was called upon to take No. 66183 from Hinksey to Newport prior to taking over on the Robeston tanks diagram. The duo is seen approaching Severn Tunnel Junction.

Since August 2017, DB Cargo has been operating two trains a day between the closed colliery at Kellingley and Killingholme on the south bank of the Humber. Waste slag is being moved from the colliery to be used in the construction of a new riverside quay. On 19 April 2018, No. 66054 leads the rake across Sudforth Lane crossing into the closed colliery site.

Fellow classmate No. 66079 *James Nightall GC* was to be found on the rear of this top and tailed working. The colliery was only a few miles from Ferrybridge Power Station. It closed at the end of 2015 and its closure marked the end of deep pit mining in the UK.

Another construction industry working sees a regular DB Cargo flow between Angerstein Wharf (Tarmac), in South East London, and Woking. On 27 April 2017, No. 66006 is seen heading the loaded working through Clapham Junction.

Another construction-related working that has been running for a number of years is the flow from Whatley Quarry to the stone terminal at Banbury Road, Oxford. On 23 February 2018, No. 66162 works the return empties south pass Hinksey Yard, south of Oxford.

The Derbyshire outpost of Peak Forest (Peak Dale) remains a DB Cargo stronghold, at least for the present. On 20 March 2018, the stabling point (adjacent to the closed station here) was home to two 'new'-liveried Class 66s, Nos 66019 and 66137, awaiting their next duties.

DB Cargo's 'new' livery went one better in this view. On the same day, No. 60015 heads a matching rake of 'new'-liveried box wagons past the stabling point on a long-established freight flow from Dowlow to Ashbury's (Manchester).

As mentioned earlier, former coal hoppers (HTAs) are finding use on stone workings out of the quarry here. In this view from Great Rocks Junction, No. 66051 can be seen running round her train, having just arrived back with a rake of these empty wagons.

On the following day, 21 March 2018, Nos 66019 and No. 66137 were seen in charge of their rakes of HTAs. Both trains were being loaded at Dove Holes Quarry for departures later that day.

Various wagon types are used on these important aggregate trains. Looking resplendent in DB Cargo's new house colours, this box wagon is designated MMA and numbered No. 7055000746 within the RIV series. It is seen passing through Doncaster.

An earlier series of DB Cargo aggregate hopper wagons was built in 2006 in Romania. These were designated HQAs and a total of sixty-eight were built, including No. 320000, the first numbered of the series. It is seen in Acton Yard.

The year 2015 also saw delivery of the first batch of aggregate wagons to be designated HOAs and branded with 'Tarmac – a CRH company'. Operating out of Mountsorrel Quarry in Leicestershire, RIV No. 7069570387 is seen passing through Bedford.

Another type of aggregate wagon is seen at Wembley Yard, resplendent in the DB Cargo (then DB Schenker) house colours. Designated HKA, and built for National Power over twenty years ago, wagon No. 300630 was in use on a sand flow between Ipswich and Watford when seen here in Wembley Yard.

The threats to DB Cargo's UK business can be seen in the next four photographs. The much broadcasted downturn in coal burning at power stations was never more apparent than in the loss of this important flow across Central Scotland. On 31 March 2015, No. 66114 is seen passing eastbound through Greenfaulds on a loaded coal train from Hunterston to Longannet. Today, the power station has closed and the coal unloading facility at Hunterston is no longer required.

These threats also come in the form of rail freight company competition. The regular movement of oil tanks from Grangemouth to Dalston in Cumbria had been in DB Cargo's hands for many years. The traffic was, however, lost to Colas Rail in 2015. On 12 June 2013, No. 66109 moves part of the day's loaded consist through Carlisle station. Both empties and loaded wagons were moved 'by instalments' to and from the compact terminal, with train marshalling taking place at nearby Kingmoor Yard.

Another established DB Cargo flow was that of the iron ore movements on South Humberside. The company handled regular flows operating between Immingham and Santon (Scunthorpe), often using its popular fleet of Class 60 locos. On 15 November 2013, No. 60063 heads west through Barnetby on a loaded working bound for Santon. The flow continues but in the hands of Freightliner.

DB Cargo Class 67s were regularly used for the delivery of Class 345 units for the new Crossrail services. On 2 May 2017, No. 67006 *Royal Sovereign* approaches Bedford while delivering No. 345007 to Wembley Yard via the Marston Vale line to Bletchley. A newer entrant into the marketplace, Rail Operations Group, now handles these deliveries.

In common with most other freight operators, DB Cargo makes a contribution to keeping trains moving during the difficult leaf fall season. These Rail Head Treatment Trains (RHTT) utilise a pair of locos operating in top and tail formation with the wagons sandwiched in between. A pair of Class 66s, Nos 66126 and 66098, pause between duties at Bristol Temple Meads on 12 October 2013.

The rail treatment, involving powerful water jets, can be seen in this view of Nos 66185 and 66058 working through Nuneaton on 23 October 2017. This particular RHTT diagram covered an area from Bescot in the West Midlands to London Euston, involving a long stretch of the West Coast Main Line. No. 66058 has since become a GBRf loco and is now numbered 66783.

During the autumn these services usually operate seven days a week. On Sunday 26 November 2017, Nos 66027 and 66127 are seen at Newton Abbot. They are reversing in the station while employed on a circular diagram based on the Cornish depot at St Blazey, near Par.

DB Cargo Class 67s also make appearances on these autumn leaf fall workings. For several years a pair has been used on the southern section of the Midland Main Line, operating to and from Toton. On 16 November 2016, Nos 67008 and 67003 are paired as they head south through Bedford.

Light engine movements are, for a number of reasons, a necessary overhead in order to have 'the right loco in the right place at the right time'. On 14 November 2014, No. 66199 makes the short move across London from Ripple Lane in the east to Acton Yard in the west. It is seen passing through Willesden Junction's High Level platforms.

On 30 June 2014, No. 66170 is involved in a much longer journey. It is heading south through Tamworth High Level on a light engine move from Doncaster to Eastleigh. It will return much later in the day with an empty rake of steel carriers destined for Scunthorpe.

Weekend engineering duties often require the movement of loco convoys in order to pick up the rakes of wagons. On Saturday 29 April 2017, four locos, which had been working in the South Wales area during the previous week, were rounded up for this move. Nos 66034, 66002, 66004 and 66093 were involved in this move from Margam to Eastleigh.

Light engine moves to and from DB Cargo's Crewe base and London's Wembley Yard take place many times a week. These can involve any combination of their loco classes. In this view taken on 6 March 2018, No. 90034 leads No. 67016 through Nuneaton. The pair are heading for Wembley Yard.

DB Cargo retains a small base in Cornwall to serve the china clay industry in the county. The allocated Class 66 loco for these workings is stabled at St Blazey Depot, near Par, usually for several months at a time. On 2 June 2016. No. 66027 is about to pass the depot with a typical loaded working from Goonbarrow to Fowey. The china clay will be loaded onto a ship at the docks there.

On 28 May 2015, No. 66188 passes through Liskeard station on a loaded rake of Imery's china clay wagons. It is heading from St Blazey to Exeter Riverside initially. The working is split to enable the loco to cope with the demands of the Devon banks, before meandering north via Newport (South Wales) and Bescot Yard en route to Cliffe Vale, Stoke-on-Trent.

On 30 May 2017, No. 66175 is seen passing through Par station, this time heading west on a working from St Blazey to Parkandillack, near St Austell.

A fleet of almost 140 wagons, designated CDAs, were originally used on these Cornish workings. This number has reduced in recent years, with just over half of that original number being available for traffic. One example, No. 375032, is shown here at St Blazey.

DB Cargo's UK fleet of Class 92 locomotives has dwindled to just six examples. These have had their shoe gear removed or isolated and are now predominantly used on Channel Tunnel and HS1 traffic. They are maintained at Crewe Electric Depot and new-liveried No. 92016 is seen there on 1 October 2017.

These six locos have, however, found occasional use on the WCML in recent years. For example, on 15 May 2015, No. 92011 *Handel* is seen heading north through Northampton with the Wembley to Daventry vans. This traffic flow is bottled water from France, which arrives in the UK via the Channel Tunnel.

A little further north at Nuneaton on 24 March 2015, No. 92042 passes southbound with the intermodal from Mossend to Daventry.

On 9 June 2017, No. 92015 hitches a lift on the rear (with Nos 90024 and 90020) as the three locos form a light engine convoy from Crewe to Wembley. They are seen southbound through Nuneaton.

This view of Tees Yard was taken on 16 April 2018, showing the somewhat forlorn sight of what is currently stabled in the North Yard, summing up the tough climate in which DB Cargo operates. Approaching 200 steel wagons have been cut up in the area over the last few months. The rakes of out-of-use DB Cargo coal hoppers are a further indication of the downturn in the company's core businesses.

With the downturn in coal and steel in particular, the importance of the aggregate traffic cannot be overstated. On 21 March 2018, No. 66051 approaches Edale with a rake of returning stone empties from Washwood Heath to Peak Forest.

On 21 September 2017, a gleaming new-liveried No. 66034 is also heading to Peak Forest. It is seen approaching Derby station with another return working from Washwood Heath.

Also heading for Peak Forest was No. 66155 on 23 April 2018. It is seen, complete with a rake of new corporate livery box wagons, returning from Ripple Lane in East London as it passes through Nuneaton.

DB Cargo claims to move 90 per cent of all finished vehicle rail movements in the UK, equating to almost a quarter of a million vehicles per annum. On 29 April 2017, No. 66067 passes Eastleigh Yard with loaded vehicles from Morris Cowley to Southampton Docks.

On 14 November 2017, No. 66128 passes close to the village of South Moreton, near Didcot, working a lengthy rake of return empties from Southampton Docks to Halewood on Merseyside.

Over the last few years, several of DB Cargo's fleet of Class 67 locos have been outshopped in a variety of liveries. In 2007, No. 67029 was named *Royal Diamond*. It is seen at Doncaster on 8 February 2017.

Reflecting a period when these locos handled Chiltern passenger services out of London Marylebone, Nos 67014 and 67012 still carried these colours when seen at Doncaster on 14 March 2018.

Another 67 involved in a royal naming was No. 67026 *Diamond Jubilee*. Its unveiling, complete with diamond jubilee design and Union Jack, coincided with HM the Queen's Diamond Jubilee celebrations in 2012. The loco is seen at Doncaster on 3 September 2015.

More recently, locos Nos 67021 and 67024 were repainted in recognition of DB Cargo's contract to haul the Belmond British Pullman. Here, No. 67021 is stabled in Wembley Yard on 5 April 2018.

A long-established steel flow links the Port of Immingham and the steel terminal at Wolverhampton. On 29 March 2018, No. 60007 *The Spirit of Tom Kendell* works a long rake of returning empties through Derby station.

DB Cargo has recently commenced an additional flow from Boston in Lincolnshire. This effectively replaces a service hitherto operated by Colas Rail in and out of Washwood Heath. On 10 April 2018, No. 66001 heads through Tamworth High Level working to Boston.

Another long-established flow is seen here at Conisbrough on 25 October 2017. The working is from Hull (Hedon Road) to Rotherham Steel Terminal.

One of the few remaining freight flows through the Channel Tunnel involves the movement of steel billets from Scunthorpe to Ebange in Eastern France. Here, on 16 February 2018, No. 66060 heads the return empties northwards through Newark Northgate. The loco had recently suffered from a graffiti attack.

Another one of DB Cargo's hubs that has reduced in importance in recent years is Warrington Arpley Yard. On 9 March 2018, No. 66087 approaches Crewe with a once or twice-weekly trip working from Arpley to the wagon repair depot at Marcroft, Stoke-on-Trent.

On 28 June 2017, No. 66074 heads through Stafford on another trip working from Arpley. This time the destination is Bescot Yard.

With the loss of some traffic to competitors, Scunthorpe is another DB Cargo hub experiencing a reduction in terms of the volume of traffic. On 16 March 2018, Nos 66186 and 60059 are both laying over in the yard. The local coal and iron ore flows are both handled by Freightliner at the time of writing.

There is, however, still a regular working of long welded rail from Scunthorpe to Eastleigh. On 8 June 2017, No. 66120 passes Chesterfield on the loaded southbound working.

Arguably, the two 'Royal' Class 67s are the company's top celebrities. No. 67005 *Queen's Messenger* and No. 67006 *Royal Sovereign* are the usual haulage when the company is called upon to transport the Royal Family. On 26 March 2018, No. 67005 is on the rear of the Royal Train as it heads south through Nuneaton.

Just over an hour later, No. 67006 is caught on camera leading the same working, which had travelled via the Northampton loop, as it passes through Bletchley platform.

DB Cargo is one of only two or three companies to operate steam locomotives on charter services on the main line, utilising its operating licence. Sometimes, these require steam loco light engine moves and are occasionally accompanied by one of their diesels. On 15 February 2018, No. 66158 fronts No. 46100 *Royal Scot* as the pair heads north through Nuneaton on a move from Southall to Crewe.

On the East Coast Main Line on 17 June 2017, No. 66047 is paired with No. 60009 *Union of South Africa* on a light engine move from the National Railway Museum at York to Stewarts Lane in London. They are seen here at Tempsford crossing, north of Sandy.

The long-established trains operated for Plasmor Ltd connect their facilities at Heck (near Goole), Biggleswade (Bedfordshire), and Bow in East London. On 30 June 2017, No. 66001 works the return empties from Bow to Heck. The train is passing through Peterborough.

In total contrast, a brand-new trial operated by DB Cargo ran in 2017. It covered in excess of 7,000 miles travelling from Yiwu (South East China) to London, crossing ten countries on its journey to Barking. To mark the occasion, No. 66136 was suitably branded for the occasion. On 14 November 2017, the loco is seen on a much lower-profile service – empty box wagons from Oxford to Whatley.

Greater Anglia have occasionally hired in Class 90 locos from DB Cargo. This usually occurs when they have a shortage within their own fleet of fifteen of these locos. On 16 June 2016, No. 90034 propels a London Liverpool Street to Norwich service as it heads north out of Ipswich.

Class 90 No. 90028 was called upon to lead a more unusual light engine move on 20 March 2017. It was giving a lift to No. 59103 *Village of Mells* from Crewe to Wembley. The Class 59 had been to Crewe for tyre turning and was returning to its home territory.

DB Cargo also makes occasional use of its so-called Management Train. This consists of three coaches and a Driving Vehicle Trailer (DVT) and is usually hauled by a Class 67. No. 67029 *Royal Diamond* is the preferred choice of traction and was in use when seen here passing south through Chesterfield on 7 September 2012.

Similarly, the Management Train usually operates with its own dedicated DVT, numbered 82146. On 13 April 2018, it is stabled along with the rest of the rake in Humberstone Road sidings in Leicester.

Acton Yard is one of the most important DB Cargo hubs in the UK. The aggregate traffic serving London and the Home Counties is split and joined in this West London yard for onward movement to and from the West Country quarries of Whatley and Merehead. These workings arrive at Acton from the west as so-called 'jumbo' trains. On 19 June 2015, this is the typical scene as Nos 59205 and 66079 *James Nightall GC* face east waiting their turn to join the North London Line.

On 5 April 2018, Nos 66018 and 66154 are seen facing west at the opposite end of Acton Yard.

On 5 April 2018, two DB Cargo workings head east within 15 minutes of each other. First, No. 66068 is about to take the North London Line (NLL) working from Calvert to Wembley.

Secondly, No. 66183 is waiting the signal to take the NLL working from Park Royal, in West London, to Hither Green, south of the Thames.

Those yards that remain on the rail network are for shared use. At Hoo Junction on 14 December 2017, for example, DB Cargo's No. 66131 reverses into the yard with a rake of ageing four-wheeled hopper wagons. It is seen passing a GBRf Class 66 awaiting its next duty.

Similarly, the track yard at Beeston, near Nottingham, is regularly served by Direct Rail Services as well as DB Cargo. On 19 April 2017, No. 66155 is seen shunting in the yard as it assembles a return working destined for Toton Yard.

As already mentioned, Toton is an operational hub for DB Cargo loco stabling and servicing, although its future had been in doubt. It now appears that, as recently as March 2018, agreement had been reached for the HS2 project to progress in the Toton area without directly impacting on DB Cargo's operations. The yards are often used for weekend stabling of rakes of wagons as well as locomotives. In this view on Friday 22 July 2016, No. 66200 heads north through Bedford on a rake of empty cement wagons from St Pancras Churchyard Sidings. The rake would ordinarily return to the company's base at Ketton, Rutland; instead, the wagons will lay over at Toton Yard during the weekend.

The importance of Toton as a weekend engineering base is evident in this view. On 28 January 2017, Nos 66130, 66031 and 66011 are all waiting to leave on infrastructure trains. No. 66207 is also about to pick up its train.

On 21 May 2013, No. 66213 is seen passing Long Eaton as it heads south from Toton Yard on an engineering train destined for the southern end of the Midland Main Line. This particular loco is one of those now operating in France for Euro Cargo Rail.

Of those Class 66s remaining in the UK, or not sold to competitors, almost all see regular use and routine servicing. No. 66043, however, has not seen use since arriving at Toton towards the end of April 2017. Three years earlier, on 23 April 2014, it is about to leave the yard on an infrastructure working.

At the time of rail privatisation, the fleet of BR container flats passed to Freightliner. In 2000, EWS therefore ordered 200 pairs of container flats, designated FCAs, to be built by Thrall at York for their own intermodal traffic. Wagon No. 610396 is seen here at Leicester.

The overall finish size of shipping containers has since been increased, giving the company a problem, and resulting in a number of these flats finding more suitable work. One such use has been on the binliner service between Knowsley and Wilton. Wagon No. 610032 is seen near York on this working.

Around the same time, EWS ordered 150 twin megafret wagons, designated FKAs. One example, wagon No. 7049080044, is seen here at Carlisle in the consist of a Malcolm Logistics Anglo-Scottish working.

DB Cargo also uses twin flats that were built in the mid-1990s and designated FIAs. Wagon No. 7049385335 is seen in this consist at Leamington Spa.

The importance of Southampton's traffic to DB Cargo is highlighted in these two workings. First, on 21 March 2015, No. 66175 has just left Trafford Park for Southampton Docks as it makes use of the through platforms at Manchester's Piccadilly station.

Secondly, No. 66206 has left Southampton and reached Leamington Spa in this view taken on 9 May 2017. This time the train's destination is Wakefield Euro Terminal.

Inland terminals such as Daventry are also important to DB Cargo. On 8 May 2017, a pair of DB Cargo Class 90s, Nos 90028 and 90036 *Driver Jack Mills*, is heading for Daventry on a working from Mossend.

On 15 February 2018, No. 66021 heads its train of cargowaggons south through Bletchley. This regular working is from Daventry to Dollands Moor (for the Channel Tunnel). The train will lay over in Wembley Yard.

Wembley Yard can be home to just about any combination of DB Cargo loco classes. On 26 May 2017, No. 66098 is stabled. It will shortly work north light engine to collect a rake of cargowaggons from Daventry.

A typical cluster of locos is stabled when seen on this pass of the yard later the same day. Three different classes are represented in the form of Nos 92016, 90037 and 67006.

South Wales is another stronghold for DB Cargo, as evidenced in these two inbound workings to Margam Yard. First, On 1 July 2017, No. 66103 passes Codsall (between Shrewsbury and Wolverhampton) returning from Dee Marsh to Margam.

Secondly, No. 66095 passes through Cardiff Central's platform on 9 November 2017. It's almost at journey's end after a long trip cross country from Tees Yard.

Margam Yard dispatches workings throughout the country. First, on 16 July 2015, No. 66113 heads a long rake of assorted steel wagon types towards Cardiff Central on a working to Dollands Moor.

Secondly, No. 66152 *Derek Holmes – Railway Operator* has almost completed its winding path across the country to reach Corby. On 10 October 2014, it heads south through Loughborough with its load of steel coils.

DB Cargo usually rosters pairs of its Class 67s for charter workings. On 7 June 2017, No. 67015 is leading a Victoria to Chesterfield working (for nearby Chatsworth House) as it heads north through Bedford.

More unusual is the use of No. 66013 as its partner, on the rear as it heads north. Class 66s are less common on these charters, although some of these specials are designed specifically to cater for the 'Shed' enthusiast railtour market.

Sometimes, competitors can cooperate. On 12 February 2018, DB Cargo's No. 66037 is given a lift from Westbury to Bescot. The working is in the hands of Colas Rail Class 70 No. 70816.

More often, competition is more aggressive and this working is a good example, having been lost to Colas Rail and now, seemingly, won back by DB Cargo. The working involves delivery of jet fuel to Rolls-Royce's test plant at Derby. The service runs from Grangemouth to Sinfin and the return working is seen here on 17 April 2018 as it passes Shipton, just north of York.